# Can God Create a Rock He Cannot Lift?: Omnipotence Paradox

ahmet yazici

Published by ahmet yazici, 2022.

CAN GOD CREATE A ROCK HE CANNOT LIFT?: OMNIPOTENCE PARADOX

**First edition. September 16, 2022.**

Copyright © 2022 ahmet yazici.

ISBN: 979-8215719879

Written by ahmet yazici.

# Table of Contents

To Muhammad Samir, Ahmet Shakir, Engin Demir,
Adem Kandemir, Bedirhan Kaldirim...

# Introduction

It is forbidden to speak or think about the Essence of God Almighty, or to dream up the image, shape, or appearance of Allah the Almighty. We are permitted to think only of His attributes, and we can learn about the Almighty through His names and attributes. In this context, I attempted to answer the above question. Such inquiries can be multiplied.

-Can God kill himself?

-Can God create another God?

-Who created God?

...

I've also made an effort to provide succinct responses to these questions. If you encounter such questions, consider these answers to be a template that can be applied to all of them.

Mankind has the ability to create an item out of matter. But he can't make anything out of nothing. He is also incapable of annihilating anything. In contrast, God's infinite power is capable of creating something from nothing and annihilating it. If He so chooses, the entire universe will be plunged into darkness right now. Any increase or decrease in His absolute power, regardless of how much He creates, is unimaginable. Is there anything, then, that would make such power insufficient?

# Why Did God Not Create A Better Universe?

Divine wisdom created this universe step by step. It is not the result of God's incompetence. He could certainly create a tree in an instant if He so wished. However, numerous pearls of wisdom would not occur in this case. In this world, Al-Hakeem predominates, but Al-Qadir will predominate in the afterlife. As a result, everything in paradise will be created in an instant.

This world is perfect in terms of the visible world's standard of living. The human being is the final and most perfect creature. He was made the Caliph of the Earth. There is no difference whether he is Muslim, Christian, Jewish, or atheist. The human being is a small universe, and the universe is a great human being. Everything in our universe is interconnected. We cannot conceive of a perfect world than this visible one. Of course, the conditions in the Hereafter are vastly different. It is far more beautiful than our planet.

Al-Hakeem: The Perfectly Wise

Al-Qadir: The All Powerful

The God Almighty neither waste nor excess while creating. This is the manifestation of Al-Adl. He gives everyone their exact right. In this world, there are manifestations of the name of Al-Adl just like other names and attributes of God Almighty.

Thus, our earth was created in perfect form. While Human being designs a technological product imitates God's arts. Man is incapable of making something, having higher quality than God Almighty created. The Almighty God creates just one time; on the contrary, the human being needs to develop his products constantly.

This world is a trial and testing area. It was created optimally for this purpose.

Moreover, this world is a great manifestation of the names and attributes of God.

As a conclusion, there are a lot of wisdom and purposes of the creation of the universe. We cannot know it. It's enough to understand that God is All-powerful, All-wise, and freed from all incompetence, as observing this world and around.

Al-Adl: The Just

# Can God Create A Rock So Heavy That He Cannot Lift It?

This question and other questions similar to this contain a great contradiction.

Let us give an answer it both yes and no:

"No, He can't."

"How can He be a god if He cannot create anything?"

"Yes, He can."

"How can He be a god if He is unable to carry or lift this rock?"

That is, this question is illogical.

To understand this better, we need to open the question:

The real problem: Can "Omnipotent One" create a rock He cannot lift?

This question is sophism; no mind can believe that a creature is greater than God. It is demagogic fallacy which has unrealistic comparisons. Just as: When a Demagog sees a plane picture, he says: All planes fly, so this plane flies too.

This question primarily contains many oddities. It is acknowledged that the entity that is intended to be created does not currently exist. It is acknowledged that God is the Creator and that this hypothetical entity will be a creature since it is expected that God created it. They also desire that Allah (SWT) will grant that imaginary entity greatness, power, and perfection.

Even though that imaginary entity is needy, helpless, weak, and needs to be created, it is asked whether the imaginary being is greater than God Almighty who is Eternal, the only Creator, Everlasting and Absolute Power owner.

The question is based on contradictory judgments. Hence, this question is not valid and has no logical and scientific value. Such questions do not deserve an answer. Because they are illogical and absurd. "Can God create a rectangle in the shape of a circle or a circle in the shape of a triangle?" A rectangle is a rectangle. A triangle is a triangle. They are called so because of their shapes. These kinds of questions are contradictory in themselves. For example: "Can a larger number be written than infinity?" It cannot be imagined a larger number than infinite. For this reason, this is based on contradictory judgments as well. Because infinite is a symbol of boundless greatness, no number can be compared to infinity. If a number is larger than infinity, then the contradiction and impossibility of being a finite number greater than infinity ensues. Likewise; if a creature is greater than the God Almighty, the meaning and attribute of the Divinity disappear.

At this point, let's reveal the difference between intellectually impossible and customarily impossible. Even though it is customarily impossible for water to gush out of a person's fingers, it is definitely not intellectually impossible. (It is a miracle of our Prophet (PBUH).) Because the mind allows it to be imagined.

Therefore, no prophet's miracle is rationally impossible, but it is traditionally considered impossible. Customarily impossible things are actually possible. And things that are intellectually impossible consist of thoughts and illusions that the mind produces (or even cannot produce) and that cannot exist in the external world.

It is impossible for a work to exceed the perfection of its master or for an architect to do a work beyond his own craft. Likewise; creatures cannot exceed the perfection of the God Almighty.

The question also refers this: "Is Allah able to give more than his own perfection to a creature?"

Badiuzzaman Said Nursi evaluates this subject as follows: "Just as the body relies on the spirit and subsists through it and is animated by it, and a word looks to the meaning and is illuminated by it, and form relies on reality and acquires value through it; so this corporeal and material manifest world is a body, a word, a form which relies on the Divine Names behind the veil of the Unseen, receiving life and vitality from them; it looks to them, and is beautified. All the instances of physical beauty proceed from the non-physical beauties of their own realities and meanings; and as for their realities, they receive effulgence from the Divine Names and are shadows of them of a sort. This truth is proved decisively in the Risale-i Nur.

This means that all the varieties and sorts of beauty in the universe are the signs, marks, and manifestations —by means of names— of a faultless, transcendent Beauty which is manifested from beyond the veil of the Unseen. However, since the

Necessary Existent's Most Pure and Holy Essence resembles absolutely nothing at all and His attributes are infinitely superior to the attributes of contingent beings, His sacred beauty also does not resemble the beauties of creatures and contingent beings, and is infinitely more exalted. Certainly, an everlasting beauty one manifestation of which is vast Paradise together with all its exquisiteness and beauty, and one hour's vision of which makes the inhabitants of Paradise oblivious to it cannot be finite, nor have any like, equal or peer.

It is clear that the beauties of a thing are in accordance with itself; and there are thousands of sorts of beauties which all differ according to the different sorts of beings. For example, beauty perceived by the eye is not the same as something beautiful heard with the ears, and an abstract beauty comprehended by the mind is not the same as the beauty of food relished by the tongue; so too, the beauties appreciated and perceived as beautiful by the external and inner senses and the spirit are all different. For example, the beauty of belief, the beauty of reality, the beauty of light, the beauty of a flower, the beauty of spirit, and the beauties of form, compassion, justice, kindness, and wisdom. Similarly, since the utter and infinite beauties of the Most Beautiful Names of the All-Beauteous One of Glory are all different, the beauties in beings also differ."

# The Attributes of Allah

There are impossibilities of this question as the number as of God's acts and attributes. When we know God by his attributes, we can have no hesitation about his presence and unity. I have tried to denote below that they sound nonsense to what extent if we look at such questions from the perspective of attributes of Allah. Let us list some of them as an example.

# a) Qudrah (Power)

It goes as follows:

"Can the Almighty, the Eternal Power, create someone more powerful than himself?"

The owner of this problem is ignorant of the notion of infinity. There is no greater power than eternal power. The God Almighty's power is limitless; nothing lessens from His eternal power, even if He creates billions of universes.

A quote from Risale-i Nur Collection by Badiuzzaman Said Nursi related to issue:

"That is, Divine power is such that it is powerful over all things, encompasses all things, is essential to the Necessarily Existent One, and according to logic, is "necessary" to Him; it is impossible that it should be separated from Him; there is no possibility that it could be. Since the Most Pure and Holy Essence possesses such necessary power, impotence, its opposite, could certainly in no way intervene in it. Impotence could not impinge on the All-Powerful Essence. Since the existence of degrees in a thing occurs through the intervention of its opposite —for example, the degrees and levels of heat occur through the intervention of cold, and the degrees of beauty, through the intervention of ugliness— impotence, the opposite of this essential power, can in no way approach it; there is no possibility whatsoever that it could. There can be no degrees in that absolute power. Since there can be no degrees in it, stars and particles are equal to that power, and there are no differences for it between the part and the whole, or an individual and a species. The raising to life of a seed and a huge tree, and the universe and man, and one individual and all beings with spirits at the resurrection of the dead is equal in relation to that power, and all are equally easy. There is no difference between great and small, many and few. Decisive witnesses to this truth are the perfect art, order, balance, distinction and profusion that we see in the creation of things with absolute speed, absolute ease, and complete facility."

# b) Iradah (Will of Allah)

It goes as follows:

"Can the Absolute Will create someone who bounds and limits his eternal Will?"

The Will of Allah has no beginning and no end; it is absolute, eternal. Nothing can limit his will. It is impossible for an entity to limit God's will. Nothing takes place if He does not wish. The following verse states this fact:

She said, "My Lord, how will I have a child when no man has touched me?" [The angel] said, "Such is Allah; He creates what He wills. When He decrees a matter, He only says to it, 'Be,' and it is. (Ali-Imran, 3:47)

On the other hand, the thing that Allah Almighty creates becomes a creature. The created being is under the Will and control of the Creator. With this question, it is assumed that the Will of the Creator is limited and the will of the creature is unlimited. Thus, a big contradiction is in question here.

# c) Pre-eternity and Post-eternity

"Can Almighty create an entity that exists before Himself and will continue to exist after Himself?"

There is a paradox in this question. The God Almighty has no beginning and ending. There is no time beyond pre-eternity and post-eternity. How possibly a creature could be pre-eternal and immortal in spite of existing later. Or the Eternal Creator could be a creature being and mortal in spite of having no beginning and end.

Suppose a computer had a conscious and mind, if we asked it about its manufacturer, it would probably say that: "he has components like wire, screen, keyboard, etc." However: It could not comprehend the nature of the human being. Likewise; we are limited from all aspects, and we are bound to space, time, matter, appearance, shape, color, etc. However; our Creator is not like the universe and us. Just as a computer cannot be like his manufacturer, God Almighty cannot resemble those who created later. He cannot be compared with anything.

# d) Al-Qayyum (The Self-Existing One)

Can God Almighty create another God to keep Himself alive and could He be dependent on another being?

Al-Qayyum means The One who remains and does not end. Every single thing in the universe needs the God Almighty to exist. He sustains the whole universe and everything in it. He is not who created the universe and let it alone; He creates every moment. For example; if electricity is cut off by the power plant of a city, the whole city is plunged into darkness. Likewise; Al-Qayyum sustains every single particle of the universe. It cannot be imagined even one moment in the universe that Al-Qayyum does not act. He creates in every single moment. The movements of the particles are like the tip of the destiny pen. Just as a bulb flashes on and off many times in a second. But we cannot understand this occurrence as it happens much faster than our visual ability. Similarly; the universe is disappearing every moment, and coming into being again. But this event takes place so perfectly that we cannot notice.

Al-Qayyum: The Self-Existing One

BADIUZZAMAN SAID NURSI refers to Al-Qayyum as following:

"The universe's Glorious Creator is Self-Subsistent, that is, He subsists, continues, endures of Himself. All things subsist and continue through Him, they remain in existence and have permanence. If the relationship of Self-Subsistence were cut off from the universe for even the fraction of a second, the universe would be annihilated.

Furthermore, as the Qur'an of Mighty Stature decrees, together with the Al Glorious One's Self-Subsistence,

There is nothing that is like unto Him. (42:11)

That is, He has no like, equal, peer, or partner in either His essence, or His attributes, or His actions. Indeed, it is not possible for the Most and Holy One who holds the universe with its circumstances and functions in the grasp of His dominicality and regulates, administers, sustains and nurtures it with perfect order as though it were a house or a palace to have any like, equal, partner, or peer; it is impossible.

Yes, it is indeed impossible that the All-Glorious Ever-Living and Self-Subsistent One for whom the creation of the stars is as easy as that of particles; to whose power the greatest thing is subjugated as is the most minute; for whom nothing is an obstacle to any other thing and no action obstructs any other action; in whose view innumerable individuals are present in the same way that a single individual is present; who hears all voices simultaneously and is able to answer the limitless needs of all simultaneously; outside the sphere of whose will and volition is nothing, no state, as is testified to by the order and balance of the beings in the universe; who although He is in no place, is present everywhere through His power and knowledge; and although everything is utterly distant from Him, is utterly close to them – that He should have any like, equal, partner, deputy, opposite or peer is not possible; it is impossible. His sacred qualities and attributes can be considered only through allegory and comparison."

Other names and attributes of the Almighty God can be considered in the same logic and measure framework.

Our first duty in the world is to know and recognize Allah (SWT). There is no limit in the path of recognizing Him in consequence of his endless attributes. When we proceed on this path, we can become a real human being. To recognize Him by the conditions of the world is the original purpose of man's creation. Otherwise, on the day of Judgment, no one who does not know Him will remain.

# Absolute Dominance of Allah Rejects Partner or Rival

———

Badiuzzaman states this fact splendidly:

"If there were in the heavens and the earth other gods besides God, there surely would have been confusion in both. Everything will perish save His countenance; His is the command, and to Him shall you return.

This is the Window of the scholars of theology (kalam), based on contingency and createdness, and their highway for proving the Necessarily Existent One. For all the details, we refer you to the scholars' great books like Sharh al-Mawaqif and Sharh al-Maqasid, and here only demonstrate one or two rays which spill on the spirit from the effulgence of the Qur'an and this Window. It is as follows:

It is the requirement of dominion and rulership not to accept rivals; they reject partnership; they repudiate interference. It is because of this that if there are two headmen in a village, they will destroy its tranquillity and order. Or if there are two chief officials in a district, or two governors in a province, they will cause chaos. Or if there are two kings in a country, they will cause complete and stormy confusion. Since a pale shadow and petty example of dominion and rulership in impotent human beings needy for assistance does not accept the interference of rivals, opponents, or peers, then you may compare how fully a rulership which is in the form of absolute sovereignty and a dominion at the degree of dominicality will enforce that law of the rejection of interference in One Possessing Absolute Power. That is to say, the most definite and constant necessity of Godhead and dominicality are unity and singleness. The clear proof and certain testimony to this are the perfect order and beautiful harmony in the universe. There is such an order from the wing of a fly to the lamps in the heavens that the intellect prostrates before it in wonder and appreciation, declaring: "Glory be to God! What wonders God has willed! How great are God's blessings!" Had there been an iota of space for partners to God, and had there been interference, as the verse, If there were in the heavens and the earth other gods besides God, there would have been confusion in both indicates, the order would have been destroyed, the form changed, and signs of disorder would have appeared. But as the verses,

"So turn your vision again: do you see any flaw? Then turn your vision a second time; your vision will come back to you in a state dazzled and truly defeated."

state and point out, however much the human gaze tries to find faults, it can find none anywhere, and returns worn out to its dwelling, the eye, and says to the fault-finding mind who sent it: "I am worn out for nothing; there are no faults." This shows that the order and regularity are most perfect. That is to say, the order in the universe is a definitive witness to Divine unity."

# The Rule of Non-Coexistence of the Opposites

Another point is it is impossible for a truth to turn into its opposite and to maintain its own nature. Two opposites are impossible to coexist.

For example, White color cannot turn into black without losing its whiteness or a sheep cannot be a wolf at the same time. Could a room be both very hot and very cold at the same time? Or could a person be both the best and the worst in the world? Would a house be both bright and dark at the same time?

It is impossible to exist two completely opposite adjectives on something like above. Because the existence of one; already mean the absence of another.

It is surely impossible to think of such a thing about God Almighty if it cannot be imagined such a thing even about the creatures.

With the above question, it is imagined infinite truths of divinity to turn into its opposite. It is like: The imaginary entity being which is in need of creation, lacking, mortal, helpless, impotent is turned into the endless power and perfection. The Omnipotent one will be impotent; the impotent, dependent creature will be Omnipotent. It is impossible that the Absolute Perfection of God turns into helplessness, weakness. There is no level of weakness in the Sacred Presence of Allah Almighty.

Power is eternal and everlasting Attribute of the God Almighty. Namely; Attributes like powerlessness, weakness, incapable cannot be considered for Him.

Such as the light and heat are essential for the Sun, that is to say; without light and heat, the Sun is not actually the sun. They are Sun's obligatory attributes of the sun, and we cannot imagine the Sun being cold and dark. Likewise; it is obligatory to believe Allah (SWT) with His Eternal and Everlasting Power, Knowledge and other Attributes. All are essential for Him. It cannot be imagined the opposite.

Here a question may come to mind. Why does man have both power and helplessness? Is not that the two opposites coming together?

The human being has just relative power, knowledge, will, etc. We are just like a mirror and reflecting God's power. However; we are not taking a little part of God's power. Our power and knowledge are not a part of his Absolute Power. We are reflecting his power according to our mirrors size. In a mirror, the innumerable image can exist but all images are not like one original. They are also not the same kind. We have a relative power and knowledge in order to know the incomparable One. As a result; He has absolute Power; we are absolute weak. The fictitious power and other attributes of humankind indicate the One who has absolute and infinite Power and attributes.

MOREOVER, ALL OTHER qualities given us is for know Him. For example; just as we sweep and clean our home; so Allah sweeps and cleans everywhere in the universe. So we understand the name of Al-Quddus of Allah (SWT).

The perfect art of Allah (SWT) is the human being. Because he gave us the wisdom so that we could know Him by looking at the manifestations of his names and attributes. But as mentioned before, it is forbidden to think about his Sacred Essence.

CAN THE SUN TURN INTO an ocean while preserving its own nature? Can a person become a horse without ever losing his humanity? What if one day it was announced as breaking news that the Atlantic Ocean had turned into honey? Of course, it is impossible for an ocean to turn into honey while preserving its nature. While it is impossible for realities to turn into their opposites for creatures, can such a thing be thought of for Allah Almighty?

AL-QUDDUS: THE HOLY

# The Levels of Existence

The answer to this question depends on the three concepts being known. These are " (God) whose existence is a necessity, contingent (possible) and impossible" concepts. Logically, other than these three options are unthinkable.

The necessarily existent is the existence of God. His existence does not depend on any other being. His existence depends on His own being. The opposite of existence, that is, non-existence cannot be considered about God.

A quote from Risale-i Nur Collection about issue:

"If something be essential, its opposite cannot have access to the essence defined by that thing. For that would be equivalent to the union of opposites, which is an absurdity. Now with regard to this principle, since God's power is related to His Essence and is an essential concomitant of His Most Sacred Essence, impotence —the opposite of power— cannot in any way gain access to that All-Powerful Essence.

MOREOVER, THE EXISTENCE of degrees within a thing comes about through the intervention in it of its opposite. For example, strong and weak degrees of light result from the intervention of darkness; high and low degrees of heat proceed from the admixture of coldness; and greater and lesser amounts of strength are determined by the intervention and opposition of resistance. It is therefore impossible that degrees should exist in that power of the Divine Essence. He creates all things as if they were but a single thing. And since degrees do not exist in the power of the Divine Essence and it does not admit of weakness or deficiency, no obstacle can in any way obstruct it nor can the creation of anything cause it difficulty.

Since, then, nothing is difficult for God's power, He creates the supreme resurrection with the same ease as spring; spring with the same facility as a tree; and a tree with as little trouble as a flower. Further, He creates a flower as artistically as a tree; a tree as miraculously as a spring; and a spring as comprehensively and wondrously as a resurrection. All of this He accomplishes in front of our eyes."

Contingent existence means the existence of created things may or may not exist. They are not necessarily being. Existence and absence equal to it. God brought them into existence from non-existence through His will, power, and knowledge. If He wished nothing would have existed.

For a person, it is equal to write and not write a letter on paper. If he or she chooses to write, he brings the letter from non-existence into being. If he chooses not to write the letter stays in non-existence. Likewise, all the contingent beings are like a letter for the God Almighty. Everything is equal to His will and His Absolute Power. There is no small-big difference. If He wishes to create, they come into being. Otherwise; they are absent. All creatures need to God to exist and they maintain their existence with the Power and Will of the God Almighty. Unless Allah (SWT) continues to create every moment, nothing can remain.

And impossible existence means that non-existence is necessary for a being. It cannot be imagined its existence. For example; the triangle with four edges, the longest edge of the square. We can give more examples:

- A number cannot be both even and uneven.

- A number cannot be bigger than infinite.

- A man cannot sit and stand at the same time.

- A room cannot be bright and dark at the same time.

- A person's father cannot be his child at the same time.

- A car cannot move and stop at the same time.

Likewise; it is impossible that a partner or a similar to the God Almighty can exist. And it is impossible that a creature being is far superior to his Creator.

With this kind of demagogic questions, impossible existence is shown like contingent being.

LET'S IMAGINE A PERFECT statue;

"It is necessary a master making it."

"Before this statue is done, his master decides upon making a statue or not." So the master, it's contingent to do that work.

"It is impossible that the statue exceeds its Master's skill, knowledge, and power."

If we think of the same truth for the Sun:

-It is necessary that the sun possesses light. Without light, the Sun is not a Sun. Because; we know the Sun with his light, heat and seven colors.

-If the sun has a will, it is possible (contingent) to give its light to whatever it wishes.

-And it is impossible for the Sun in the mirror to have the size and temperature of the real Sun.

If considered the above examples for God:

The existence of the God Almighty is "necessary", The existence of everything that was created and is to be created is "possible." And it is absolutely "impossible" that a Godlike entity or partner or any creature to be greater and more powerful than God Almighty exist.

Allah Almighty's power is enough for everything. However, this power does not occur on absurd, unthinkable, impossible things. Allah (SWT) answers the similar question as below:

They say, "Allah has taken a son." Exalted is He! (Al- Baqarah 2:116)

He does not wish to answer this question in such a way: "No, it's not true."

We can infer from this verse that irrational things are not allowed to consider about the God Almighty.

God is infinite with all his names and attributes. That is to say, it is the same thing to create a flower or spring to God's might. There is no difference between big and small. There is no limit to his power and other attributes. With this question is wanted to give a final to this infinite power and to give infinity to a creature being whose all attributes are finite.

While infinite cannot be finite; finite cannot be infinite. That is, such a question cannot be asked.

# Pre-eternity Concept

Pre-eternity concept should be known in order to be able to understand infinite acts and attributes of God. Time is an abstract concept existing since the universe was created. It is for only creatures and divided into three parts: past, present, and future. God has no beginning and end; for this reason, there are no concepts like the present, past, and future for Him.

Pre-eternity is a confusing issue. It is not before the beginning of the time. Pre-eternity is having no past, present, and future. Pre-eternity is a concept that all times are seen at the same time. Pre-eternity is not a time and in the pre-eternity concept, there are not notions such as the past, present, future, being, space. It cannot be imagined any beginning point for pre-eternity and it is not eternal toward the past as well. Pre-eternity is that the absolute existence belongs only to Allah, who is free from time and space.

God Almighty is also free from space, appearance, and color. Allah is present everywhere but not in person; through His power, knowledge, and will. He has not any place, time, shape and does not need any of these. Those who know pre-eternity concept also knows that those questions that mentioned cannot be imagined.

# The Issue of Comparing the God Almighty with Creature Beings

The Almighty God's endless attributes and qualities cannot be compared with created one at all. His existence comes from Him, and He has no beginning and end. He is unique; he has no partner and similar. He is free of all impotence attributes and qualities and freed from time and space. If He were bound to time and space, He could not create them. Because; He existed before time and space were created. It is impossible to imagine a moment that God did not exist. If a master makes an art, he must be independent of his art, otherwise, he is not able to make it. In other words; a painter must be outside of the picture. Likewise; Allah (SWT) is independent of space and time.

Creatures are bound to time and space; they cannot exist unless God Almighty wishes to create them.

Related to this topic Badiuzzaman says:

"The human mind does not have the breadth and scope to measure divine grandeur (May He be exalted), weigh up [the Most High's] perfections, or to judge His attributes. This is not possible except in one respect - they may be gauged only from the sum total of His artefacts, and from what is manifested of all His works, and from what may be epitomized from all His acts. Yes, an atom can only be a mirror, not the measure.

If you have understood these matters, know that the Necessary Being (Be He exalted) cannot be compared with contingent beings, for they are as different from one another as are the ground and the Pleiades. Surely you can see that it was because of this false comparison, that with the Naturalists, the Mu'tazilites, and Zoroastrians their powers of delusive imagination overpowered their reasons, and they ascribed an actual effect to causes, and the creation of acts to living creatures, and the creation of evil to one other than Allâh (May He be exalted!). With their delusions and imaginings they asked how with His grandeur, sublimity, and freedom from defect (tanaz-zuh) Allâh (May He be exalted!) would condescend to [create] these base matters and ugly things. To hell with them! How could they shackle the intellect with avoid it!such a feeble delusion? But alas! As a whispering doubt it afflicts believers also. So be careful to avoid it!"

═══════════════

THE CREATOR IS INCOMPARABLE. But all comparable and relative blessings we have seen in this world indicate the greatness that cannot be compared. Moreover, different things cannot be compared to each other. But it may be possible to compare things that are the same kind.

The human mind is limited and measures everything with comparisons. For example: When we compare a horse with a cat, the horse is bigger than the cat, but when we compare the horse with an elephant, the horse loses its bigness attributes. But God Almighty's all attributes and acts are infinite. For example; for the infinite number there is no difference between one or 10 billion. It can be subtracted neither one nor 10 billion from infinite.

Those whose existence and absence are equal cannot grasp the limitless one. In other words, comparable and relative one cannot be Creator.

# Allah is Freed from Matter

Such questions can be considered about the things that have a matter. They are out of question about God. He is not material and he created the matter. No matter how big an item is supposed; it can be only compared with other material things.

When Allah's existence is compared to the other levels of existence, other beings are so pale that, some saints like Muhyiddin Ibn'ul Arabi regarded other beings as absent. Of course, the realm of existence is not an illusion. There really is. But I will not go into that topic.

This truth is declared in Risale-i Nur as following:

"His existence is essential, it is pre-eternal, it is post-eternal, its non-existence is impossible, its cessation is impossible; it is the most firmly rooted, the most sound, the strongest, and the most perfect of the levels of existence. In relation to His existence, the other levels of existence are like extremely pale shadows. The degree of Necessary Existence is so stable and real, and contingent existence is so insubstantial and pale that many of those who have investigated creation, like Muhyi al-Din al-Arabi, have reduced the other levels of existence to the level of delusion and imagination; they said: There is no existent save Him. That is, it must not be said of other things that they have existence in relation to the Necessary Existence. They stated that they are not worthy of the title of existence. "

A creature can never grasp the Creator. No matter how much a computer develops, it cannot have an idea about the manufacturer. We can only know as much as it is given to us. Moreover, we cannot grasp even our own soul.

Vision perceives Him not, but He perceives [all] vision; and He is the Subtle, the Acquainted. (Al-An'âm 6:103)

He is the First and the Last, the Ascendant and the Intimate, and He is, of all things, Knowing. (Al-Hadid 57:3)

So do not assert similarities to Allah. Indeed, Allah knows and you do not know. (An-Nahl 16:74)

Say, "If the sea were ink for [writing] the words of my Lord, the sea would be exhausted before the words of my Lord were exhausted, even if We brought the like of it as a supplement." (Al-Kahf 18:109)

And if whatever trees upon the earth were pens and the sea [was ink], replenished thereafter by seven [more] seas, the words of Allah would not be exhausted. Indeed, Allah is Exalted in Might and Wise. (Luqman 31:27)

[He is] Creator of the heavens and the earth. He has made for you from yourselves, mates, and among the cattle, mates; He multiplies you thereby. There is nothing like unto Him, and He is the Hearing, the Seeing. (Al- Shuraa 42:11)

# Can God Kill Himself?

We can also evaluate the question "Can God kill himself?" in the same frame.

The nature of Allah differs from our nature. As we mentioned before His existence is essential just as His Power. So this question is like: "Can the God Almighty end up His own existence by His own Power?" It is just like these examples: "Can man end up his imagination by his own mind or can he destroy his compassion feeling with his anger?" Can the God Almighty be both the Creator of death and also mortal? It's unimaginable. These and similar questions are a logic error. Not killing Himself is not a deficiency for Him. On the contrary, if he kills Himself, it is a defect for Him. If he dies, He cannot be God. One of the His names is Al-Hayy. He is alive. Unlike us, His life does not depend on a combination of soul, flesh or blood.

And that it is He who causes death and gives life. (An-Najm 53:44)

Al-Hayy: the Eternally Living One

# Who Created God?

This question is beside the point, but I would like to clarify it briefly. I would like to give such an example. Which of these two options can make a glass of water wetter? When you pour a bucket full of water on it or a dam full of water? Both answers are wrong. Because if wetness is essential for a thing, it also means there are no degrees of wetness; less wet or wetter is irrelevant. Likewise, it is also irrelevant to ask, "Who created God?" Because He has necessarily "Takwin" attribute, which means inventing and creating, bringing into existence out of nothing.

If you ask what made this table or coat wet? Answer is "water." Then what made water wet? How could it be possible to get the water wet?

Likewise, Sun gives the light on the planets. Then what gives the light to Sun? Such a question is nonsense.

"What's pulling the locomotive?" Can such a question be asked?

# How is God able to Do Countless Things at the Same Time?

The development of technology provides a better understanding of the truths of faith. We can understand the answer to this question to some extent by giving an example from the technology. But first I would like to start with a quote from Risale-i Nur Collection by Badiuzzaman Said Nursi:

"The degrees of existence are different. And the worlds of existence are all different. Because they are all different, a particle from a level of existence that is deeply rooted in existence is as great as a mountain from a less substantial level; it contains the mountain.

For example, the faculty of memory, which is the size of a mustard-seed in a head from the Manifest World, takes on an existence the size of a library from the World of Meaning. And a mirror the size of a fingernail from the external world encompasses a mighty city from the level of the World of Similitudes. If the memory and the mirror from the external world had possessed consciousness and creative power, they would have been able to bring about endless transformations and activity in the Worlds of Meaning and Similitudes through the power of their minute existences in the external world. That is to say, when existence is firmly established, power increases; what is only a little becomes much. Especially if having acquired complete stability existence is disengaged and detached from materiality and is not restricted, only a partial manifestation of it will be able to transform many worlds of other less substantial levels of existence."

He already clarifies the matter very well. But as I mentioned before let me give you a brief example:

Let us think a memory stick or something similar. It exists in the external world. We can put millions of image, thousands of music on it. Even though it takes the Milky Way Galaxy, the mountains and the oceans into it, its weight or shape does not change. We can suppose that the Milky Way, mountains and oceans are from the world of Meaning. We can copy, paste, delete or make a change whatever in it. Likewise; Allah's pre-eternal knowledge designs and ordains everything in the Meaning World. Then we see them in the external world. Unlike images on the memory stick, due to the fact that Allah has absolute and infinite Knowledge and Power, the slightest decrease does not occur in His Knowledge and Power.

Originator of the heavens and the earth. When He decrees a matter, He only says to it, "Be," and it is. (Al-Baqarah 2:117)

The command "Be" is given by His attributes of Knowledge, Will, and Power. We cannot think these Attributes separately.

Blessed is He in whose hand is dominion, and He is over all things competent (Al-Mulk 67:1)

# Might Angels Have Real Influence on Their Tasks?

All powers and strengths belong to Allah. Angels and other causes are only a means of the works of Allah (SWT). It's because the Dignity and Greatness of Allah (SWT) require veiling. A Governor, Chief Constable or Chief of Defence does not mingle freely with the crowd and does not perform police officers' or soldiers' jobs. Their position and dignity do not allow to this. Different from police officers, the Angels of Allah have no influence or strength. Their duty is to declare God's Power and Glory of His Divinity. Another wisdom in the creation of Angels and causes are to be a cover for deaths, misfortunes or calamities in order to prevent peoples unjust complaints reach Allah. The jobs of Angels are not a help to Allah (SWT). With fulfilling their duties, they worship to Allah. The real maker, performer, creator is only Allah.

In this world, every event takes place by causes. This is the principal and law of creation. These causes are created by Allah (SWT) as well. We cannot gain wheat unless we cultivate the soil. Neither the cloud nor the tree gives us fruit. Allah (SWT) sends all the things we need from the unseen world.

Allah is present and omnipresent everywhere, not through His Essence, but through His Names and Attributes. His Essence, on the other hand, never comes into contact with the creatures.

Influence in the material world is only possible through contact. That is, it is not possible to influence something without physically touching it. A person cannot, for example, drink a glass of water without first grasping the glass with his hand. Allah is free from this requirement. When Allah says to something, "Be," it happens instantly and without being touched. He does not have to come into contact with it in order to create something.

The actions of Almighty Allah in His creation are only by command and will. He has no personal touch. Just as the sun illuminates the universe.

Touching is a material thing. It's forbidden to think such things about Allah.

# Why is the existence of Allah not noticed?

Some things are so obvious and visible that we cannot see or notice them.

The sea is so visible that fish do not notice it. Just as we are not aware of the air even though we are always intertwined with the air...

Although the sun is so obvious, it is not very noticeable by people. Also, if we try to look at the sun with the naked eye in the middle of the day, our eyes can't stand it. The intensity of its light prevents it from being seen.

The existence of God is so clear and certain. But this certainty and clarity obscure His being seen.

Allah makes His actions so perfect that it seems as if everything happens by itself. In fact, not a single leaf falls without His permission.

# Why did Allah create things He already knew in order to see them?

Why did He create the universe and put humans to the test when He already knew?

Anyone who has beauty and perfection wishes to display their beauty and perfection. Allah wanted the beings He created to reflect His own beauty and perfection. He created the universe and the creatures for His names and attributes to appear in them.

Although everything was pre-eternally available in divine knowledge, they needed to emerge and appear on the reflecting mirrors of existence. That can only happen through the creation of beings.

Divine Determination is only concerned with knowing, or with something related to knowledge. This divine knowledge is related to our will's declaration and purpose. That is, fate knows where and how the slave will use his proclivity and will. The slave does not exercise his will because destiny is aware of it. If the slave's actions had not been created, there would be no knowledge of his doing it in his destiny.

Badiuzzaman says: "Divine Determining (destiny) is a sort of knowledge. Knowledge is dependent on the thing known. That is, it knows it as it is. The thing known is not dependent on knowledge. That is, the principles of knowledge are not fundamental so that the knowledge directs the thing known with regard to its external existence. Because the essence of the thing known and its external existence look to will and are based on power."

With His pre-eternal knowledge, Allah knows what and how His slaves will desire and act. That is what we call fate. If something is not going to happen, that is, if it is not going to be created, on what basis will it be known?

As a result, the information of something exists because it will occur. If it is not created, there will be no knowledge of its existence, but there will be knowledge of its non-existence.

Assume that a person will offer the Friday prayer next week, and Allah knows, with His pre-eternal knowledge, that His slave will do so of his own free will. Allah's knowledge of it is relevant to that slave's performing the prayer. Because he will pray, such information exists. There would be no knowledge about the slave performing the prayer if we assumed he did not do so and that the prayer was not created. Because knowing he would pray was contingent on him praying. So there was the knowledge that he would perform the Friday prayer because he was going to do so.

Allah's divine knowledge appears in how something is going to happen. If we assume that something did not happen, there would be knowing that it would not happen. If there is the knowledge that it is going to happen, it is unimaginable that it is not going to come about and not going to be created. The knowledge that something will happen depends on the fact that it will actually happen.

Knowing how something will happen in advance does not prevent it from being created; on the contrary, it increases the wish to create it. For example, if a person imagines a beautiful painting, his or her enthusiasm to paint grows.

Furthermore, creation is about more than just seeing them; Allah's wish to see the manifestations of His names and attributes is at stake. Allah says in a sacred hadith: "I was an unknown treasure and I wished to be known. So, I created the creatures." (Ajluni, Kashful-Khafa II, 132 )

# Is God in the Skies?

Almighty Allah is eternal and freed from matter. So it is not possible for Him to exist in the heavens that existed afterward. Almighty Allah is freed from space and direction. When there were no heavens, places, and direction, He existed.

# Can God Think or Decide?

Allah's pre-eternal knowledge encompasses everything that has been, is being, and will be. It is unthinkable for God to think and then decide on something. Adjectives such as noticing something later, and having a new thought cannot be conceived for Allah. Like the Essence of Allah, His Names and Attributes are also eternal/pre-eternal, and later knowledge cannot interfere with them.

Thinking is an effort to eliminate existing ignorance. It is unthinkable for Allah, the possessor of infinite knowledge, to have the attribute of ignorance at the same time.

# Is God Sitting on the Throne?

God does not sit on the throne. He does not sit on anything. If Allah is sitting on the Throne, then where was He sitting before the Throne was created?

Allah uses similes in the Qur'an. We use this type of simile a lot in our conversations. For a company, "So-and-so sat in the chair." we say. By this word, we do not mean a genuine sitting. We mean who handles the administration and who will run the business. Even if that person did not really sit in a chair, we would say the truth because this does not mean genuine sitting, but taking things over.

Likewise, for a country, we use the expression "sitting on the throne". When a monarch came to power, "So-and-so ascended the throne." we say. By this, we mean neither the true throne nor the true sitting. What we mean is that such and such a person is the ruler, he rules the state. Even if He did not sit on a throne, our word is truth.

Here, Allah Almighty has declared His dominance in this universe, that He is the sole owner of the affairs and that He is the Sultan of the whole worlds, with the verse, "(Allah) Most Gracious is firmly established on the throne (of authority) (Surah Ta-Ha, Verse 5)". The dominion of Allah (who is the Sultan of the pre-eternal and eternal), has been expressed by a simile, a metaphor in the Quran.

# Conclusion

These types of questions go through the following stages. First, they attribute characteristics to the Creator that have nothing to do with His definition. Then, the questions are based on these illogical assumptions. However, the creator is never similar to the things He creates. If they knew the concept of the Creator and deity, they would understand how absurd and funny such questions are. The expression "a stone he cannot lift" also stems from an extremely weak conception of deity.

There is a Paradox in the question:

"What happens if an unstoppable object hits a wall that can never be ruined?" This question irrational and wrong question and it has no answer. Like the questions which we have answered. It can be multiplied as follows:

-What is the longest edge of the circle?

-If one edge of the square is...

...

The reality is being confused with imagination. These questions are just imagination.

Such questions originate from not knowing the concept of greatness and Creator.

No matter how big the creature is, the size is relative to the creatures and it is considered in that category.

Allah has infinite power, and everything except Him is infinite helpless.

While it is unthinkable that a tree painting is like the original, an impotent and needy creature of Allah is being expected to be higher than Allah who is All-powerful, All-hearing, All-seeing, All-knowing, Pre-eternal, Post-eternal.

Allah (SWT) is already lifting earth, planets, galaxies, seven Heavens and above. However, there is no difference between lifting an atom and lifting the whole universe by His Absolute Power.

If something is created, it cannot be God.

If we want to know God, we must know Him the way He introduces Himself to us.

Everything is known with the opposite, and opposites (hot-cold, beautiful-ugly, bright-dark) are found together in the world. By means of opposites, the human mind can know his Creator. A man lives on the sun cannot comprehend the existence of light. Because he could not be aware of the darkness. Those who do not know darkness cannot comprehend the light. This fact is another reason there is some ugliness in this world. In this way, we can see the real beauties. A beautiful mansion or garden might have some ugly stones or some odd shapes. In this way, the mansion's and garden's beauties can be seen more vividly. If there were no cold intervention, there would not be degrees of temperature.

Since there is no weakness in God's power, there are no degrees in His Power. For this reason, He is infinite and has Absolute Power. An atom or a star is equal to his Power.

These questions bring no deficiency to God; on the contrary, they prove that Allah (SWT) is free and away from all defects and imperfections.

Allah (SWT) does not need anything. He does not need one to give Him existence because He and His attributes exist without a beginning.

The power of Allah (SWT) is absolute and unlimited but is connected to things that are rationally possible. No matter how limitless His power, it is still within the bounds of possibility. This is not a limitation of it. For example, could we ask a strong man? "Do you think you are strong? So then give birth to twins." Or is it possible for a renowned and great commander to wear a dancer's costume?

Allah does not eat, drink, or sleep. This is not a deficiency for Him. On the contrary, if He eats and drinks and sleeps, this would be a deficiency for Allah. Let me also state that Allah does not eat apples, but He knows the taste of apples with His knowledge. Allah knows every smell and every taste with His infinite and eternal knowledge. Nothing that created beings possess has ever come into existence by itself. Allah created everything. He knows everything that He created. Allah knows with His infinite knowledge the feeling of pain, toothache, crying, feeling cold, etc. However, Allah does not feel cold or pain. He knows with His knowledge.

We can infer from these questions that without God, existence is unthinkable. For example, time has started with the matter. Before matter, there was no time. The Creator of time must exist before the beginning of time. Consequently; he is freed from matter, time, shape, and so on... The question of where God was before He created the universe can also be evaluated in this context. The question of where is a valid question for creatures that were created later and are bound to a place. Since God is freed from space, a question such as "Where was God?" is illogical.

Assessing this world, we should know that everything has wisdom. Allah (SWT) does not create anything in vain. He creates everything according to a balance.

Allah (SWT) has eternal power. Power is essential for Him. Weakness is out of the question about Him. Eternal, Infinite, Absolute Power and their opposites which are the weakness, inability cannot coexist.

There is no limit to knowing God.

Knowing Allah is the opposite of knowing His existence. In other words, knowing Allah is not just about proving His existence with rational proof. To know Him with His names and adjectives is to know Him in the real sense.

Allah (SWT) has the Power over everything.

# Don't miss out!

Visit the website below and you can sign up to receive emails whenever ahmet yazici publishes a new book. There's no charge and no obligation.

https://books2read.com/r/B-A-XNWH-HCYX

BOOKS 2 READ

Connecting independent readers to independent writers.

Did you love *Can God Create a Rock He Cannot Lift?: Omnipotence Paradox*? Then you should read *Big Crunch: Invisible Apocalyptic Machines*[1] by ahmet yazici!

[2]

The Hour is near.

The countdown to the apocalypse has begun.

It's like a ticking time bomb with ten seconds to go off. That's why we experience the truth that time speeds up when the apocalypse approaches.

From time to time, different fields of the scientific world make statements such as, "A thousand years later, our earth will be in this situation; 10 million years later, the sun will be like

---

1. https://books2read.com/u/47gZRg

2. https://books2read.com/u/47gZRg

this; this country will be in this situation, etc." What if I told you that the world doesn't have a life span of 200 years?

We are about to count down to the apocalypse according to universe time.

The Prophet (PBUH) said, "The lifespan of my Ummah will not extend past 1500 years."

In this book, I attempted to describe the apocalyptic scenes described in the Qur'an and hadiths using modern astronomical discoveries and predictions (e.g., black holes, the Big Crunch...). My primary goal was to describe the apocalypse in terms of science and religion. The resulting work, however, is primarily about the secrets of the universe and the miracles of the Quran... I am confident that you will discover previously unknown secrets about the apocalypse and the universe.

I'm sure the scientific truths revealed by the Qur'an and the prophet (PBUH) fourteen centuries ago astounded you. Your astonishment will grow even stronger as you read this book.

How will the apocalypse break out? What are the possible apocalyptic scenarios with a scientific and heavenly approach?

Also by ahmet yazici

**A Glimpse into How the Universe Works**
Big Crunch: Invisible Apocalyptic Machines
An Islamic Approach to Time Travel


**A Glimpse into the Unseen Realms**
Unmaterial Molds
How to Understand the Soul: Spirit or Brain?
How Can Soothsayers Predict the Future?


**End Times, Rise of Antichrist (Dajjal), and Golden Age**
The Return of Jesus: Conquest of Rome
Armies of the Heavens: Divine Help in Wars


**Standalone**
Can God Create a Rock He Cannot Lift?: Omnipotence
Paradox

Wouldn't Eternal Life in Paradise Be Boring?: Life in Heaven
Do Humans and Apes Have the Same Ancestors?: Evolution and Creation in Light of Striking Similarities
Do All Uncovered Women Go to Hell?
Is Coronavirus a Divine Warning?
Is the Quran the Word of God?
Who Created the Mobile Phone?
Why Did Islamic Countries Lag Behind? : Is Islam Not the Right Religion?

# About the Author

Ahmet Yazici lives in Turkey with his parents and brother. He likes to write non-fiction Islamic works that prove the truths of faith in a rational way and fiction works (primarily fantasy fiction).